Leading from home

The legacy of lockdown

Tim Johns

ISBN: 978-1-8381002-0-9

"We do not receive wisdom, we must discover it for ourselves after a journey through the wilderness which no-one else can make for us, which no-one can spare us. For wisdom is the point from which we come at last to regard the world."

Marcel Proust

CONTENTS

PREFACE

This is a slim volume despite the fact that it covers a lot of ground. It's a short book because many business books are simply too long. And no one enjoys struggling through long drawn-out books. Many business books are little more than one or two big ideas padded out with interviews and case studies that stretch the original premise almost to breaking point. You don't want that. What you want is something that is to the point and easy to read.

Brevity is good. As simple as possible but no simpler.

So, if you don't want to read the whole of this book, here's the summary:

The world of work was broken long before the pandemic came along. The signs of change and the mega trends were already there. Lockdown merely accelerated them.

The world will not return to exactly as it was. And neither will work. And so working from home will continue to play a significant part in the lives of many people.

Leading from home is not the same as leading from an office. It needs new behaviours and new attitudes. But before leaders can learn to lead from home, they need to learn to lead themselves.

Leading your team from home isn't easy. So I've set out some ideas to help.

Leading your business needs to change as well. Because society has changed and so you need to refashion your business to meet the new challenges.

As a leader, you have a responsibility beyond your organisation. You can help make the world a better place.

This book aims to make you think differently and challenge your assumptions. It will help you find a better way.

Because what got you to where you are now won't help you get where you need to go.

If all that sounds interesting, please read on…

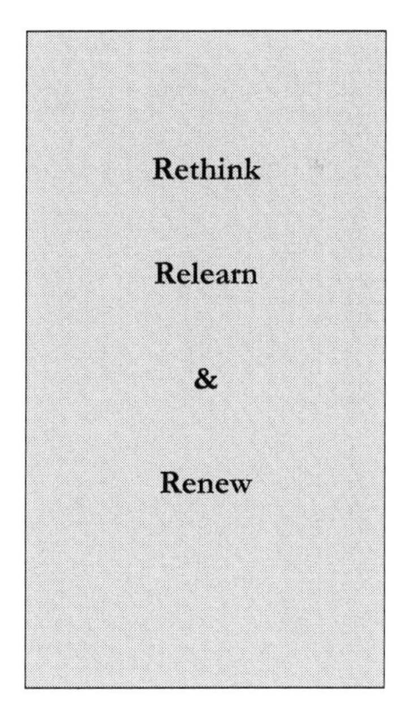

1 INTRODUCTION

If ever there was a golden age of leadership then we've probably just been through it. After years of trying to find a steady model for running organisations, the last decade seemed pretty good. Things were in a groove. All organisations were pretty much designed the same way. Executive teams all had similar responsibilities. Leadership was often multi-site and multi-country with plenty of travel. It was pretty flexible in that you could work from an office and from a hotel, thanks to always-on technology and always-on teams.

Leaders all had similar thoughts, thanks to reading the same leadership books and attending the same business school courses. Whether it was employees as the greatest asset, the importance of purpose, or the need for stakeholder engagement, more often than not a panel of leaders speaking at business conferences would all be in violent agreement.

And there was huge similarity in the playbooks. Thanks to a culture of benchmarking, everybody was doing the same things: outsourcing, shared services, buybacks – pretty much every initiative could be cut and pasted from somewhere else. And the rewards were great too.

Then Covid-19 came along followed swiftly by lockdown. In the first flush, the response was of that to a crisis. Both people and businesses went from the top of the Maslow Hierarchy of Needs (self-actualisation and purpose) to the bottom (safety and security). Then the wartime spirit kicked in. People started to think more clearly and help each other.

And then the adrenaline of dealing with the initial response wore off and there came a realisation that the impact of lockdown was going to be more profound and would last longer than people had imagined. With that came even more fear and frustration as the practicalities of the new order became clearer.

Everybody had to adjust to the new reality. Even those who had previously dabbled in the occasional working from home had to change their mindsets and their behaviours. Working from home made people act and think differently. The dislocation caused by lockdown was profound. The traditional levers of the organisation proved to be less effective. Teams and methods of reporting and managing no longer worked the way they used to. The old ways of control and reward struggled to produce the same results. And the issues were too profound to be papered over with a few quick fixes and required more than Band-Aid. And that's because the issues fell into two big categories: the physical and the mental.

Physically working from home is obviously different. The separation from the office, from co-workers and colleagues, and from the normal way of operating, meant that systems, processes and timescales all had to be rethought. The reality of working remotely, within the space and technology limitations that many people had, proved to be complex.

Mentally, the issues are just as profound. Everyone went through similar emotions. Fear was a big problem. And it wasn't just the fear of the illness. People were rightly concerned about their jobs, their families and their long-term prospects. It was hugely unsettling. It was discombobulating. Children couldn't go to school or take exams. Plans for holidays, weddings, birthdays were all cancelled. Some people were living in tough circumstances, sharing confined spaces with difficult people. Instances of domestic abuse rose. Mental health was a serious problem. These frightened and uncertain people were your colleagues, your employees and your co-workers.

The lockdown brought lots of things into sharp focus. Many realised that work was probably not the most important thing in their lives. Their families and their health were their number one priority.

As always, people looked to their leaders. Some leaders proved great in the crisis scenario but many were slow to realise that everything had to change and that included how they led. There was little in their past to guide them. In the past there was the authentic leader, the purposeful leader, the strategic leader, the visionary leader, the innovative leader and the mindful leader.

The leadership books they'd read and the courses they'd been on didn't include leading from home. The assumption was always that the captain was either on the bridge, on the shop-floor, flying between meetings, or speaking on a panel at Davos. Curiously, leading teams from a spare bedroom wasn't covered. Until now.

The legacy of lockdown

Whatever the various outcomes of the crisis turn out to be, it is likely that remote working will figure more heavily in working lives. There will always be a place for offices, just as there can never be a substitute for human interaction. But working from home is clearly going to play a significant part in the normal way of working for many people. It's not going to go away for ever. And just because it may have been forced on many of us doesn't mean that it can't provide an opportunity. An opportunity to rethink, readapt and relearn. How can we make work better and what sort of leadership do we need to make it successful.

When it comes down to it, a leader is a dealer in hope. They're people who can provide direction - a vision for the future. They help make sense and meaning. And they help overcome fear

But to do this, leaders need to be trusted. They need to connect with their people on an emotional level. Rational arguments won't work. Empathy is needed and not cold logic.

Leading a team can be tough at the best of times. But in periods of such extraordinary uncertainty it is tougher still. People will only give you permission to be led by you if they trust you.

Never let a good crisis go to waste, as the famous quote has it. The legacy of lockdown is that it provides a real opportunity to consider better ways to work. And introducing better ways to work requires better ways to lead.

Leaders need to rethink, relearn and renew.

2 WORK AS IT USED TO BE

Let's take a moment to think about work. It is extraordinary to think of how much our lives have been dominated by the office. For many people, work was somewhere you went rather than what you did. Indeed, we all know people who answered the "what do you do" question by first saying where they worked.

Offices have been the norm for many decades. They've represented the physical manifestation of a business. From banks to tech firms, pharma to ad agencies, businesses have proudly proclaimed their brands from the roof top. On the inside, offices were where the action was: a living, breathing corporate culture. They've always been the place where work was allocated, organised and processed.

But despite the vast number of offices, those of us who have visited countless companies will tell you that whatever people may say, all offices are pretty much alike. Regardless of the sector, the age of the company or its stated culture and values, they're all pretty much the same. It could be argued that the reason for this homogeneity is that they've evolved to be efficient. It's actually an interesting conundrum. Are offices designed around work or is work designed around the office?

The many advances in society haven't really changed the office that much. In the 1950s they may have had typing pools and tea trolleys but we've now got breakout rooms and free fruit. It would be a mistake to think that because we use computers and smart phones that we're both more advanced and more productive. In fact, in many senses we're less productive.

Some will say that offices are now more democratic; that there's now less distinction between managers and employees. But many are still very hierarchical. There are closed offices, albeit now with glass walls, meeting rooms, different size desks and, for some, the Executive Suite. Workers are often grouped by teams, functions and, more often than not, reporting lines. Silos are still common.

Open plan was seen as the way forward. By breaking down barriers they were meant to create an egalitarian atmosphere; a creative hub where everyone could share and be part of one big team. In reality, they are noisy places, with loud voices, telephones ringing, printers printing and uninvited people hanging around your desk. Extroverts tend to like them and introverts tend not to. If you like to shout loudly in the hope that everyone gets to hear how great you are, then open plan is the place for you.

If, however, you've actually got any serious work that requires focused thinking then they're rubbish. The myth of multitasking is a myth. If you need to focus your attention on detailed work, then the last thing you need is any distraction. It's difficult to imagine Einstein coming up with much if he had had to sit between three people sitting on bean bags talking about brand essence and two others playing pinball.

And then came hot desking. Five minutes wandering round looking for a spare desk. Five minutes to fix up the phone/laptop combination. Five minutes to get the family photos, favourite mug, succulent plant into the correct feng shui harmony. And then you find yourself next to the CEO. Nothing good can come from that arrangement.

Desks are actually very important for many people. They act as a sort of home from home. Many desks reflect the personalities of their owner: family photographs, favourite pens, baseball gloves. It represents a form of nesting, bringing a human touch to often impersonal surroundings. We can all be very territorial about our desks and feel a mild sense of violation if others impinge on our personal space. It's as if we all need to assert our independence and stand out from the crowd.

Offices are good for many things. It can be very helpful to have teams together in one place. Co-creating and co-producing can be more effective when people are together. We're social animals and like being with others. We are also instinctively tribal and an office environment can help give us a shared sense of identity. And the enforced absence of lockdown has, perhaps, given a false sense of nostalgia. Perhaps we mourned the loss of the wrong things for the right reasons.

Offices, in their current incarnation, have probably passed their use-by date. They're not entirely fit for purpose. They often encourage the wrong sorts of attitudes – eg deference, hierarchies – and the wrong sorts of behaviours – eg presenteeism

Technology is another issue. Much has been written about how IT technology was meant to liberate but how it seems to have merely enslaved. Work can often seem little more than sending, receiving, acknowledging and replying to emails.

And who hasn't been shocked to receive an email from a colleague sitting a few desks away which could and should have been a conversation, only to reflect that it's something that we've all been guilty of.

Nowadays, communication technology is so pervasive that there can be no escape. This invasion of work into home life is a serious problem for many people. It is a cause of increased stress and anxiety. We all know only too well the level of expectation for an immediate reply to an email or message at whatever time of day or night.

Being always on seems to be a sign of commitment. It's actually become a form of bullying – "I'm working so I expect you to be as well". And it affects sleep patterns, especially if both the last thing you do at night and the first thing that you do in the morning is to check messages.

And what about the concept of office hours? Nine to Five. Monday to Friday. It seems so nostalgic to look back fondly on those days. The days when there really was a demarcation between work and home. Work/life balance really did mean leaving the office behind without technology constantly following you around.

> An office worker from the 1950s would be appalled at how we've allowed computer technology to extend our working hours and blur the distinction between work and home

Of course, going to the office means some form of commute. Some people spend their commute in cars, queuing at the same traffic lights and junctions every day. Some have the pleasure of forcing themselves onto already packed underground trains. And the very brave cycle on busy roads. Some people really hate their commute.

But, it has to be said, one of the things people miss most when they work from home is the commute. This is because it can act as a buffer. It is a chance to decompress. Some read, some watch movies or play games and some doze. Having no break between work and home is a serious issue for home workers, a subject to which we will return.

The end-to-end production of a piece of work can involve a significant amount of input from outsourcing, off-shoring, agencies, advisors, partners and consultants. Few businesses can operate entirely with services that they themselves provide from within their own office.

And yet offices dominate the skylines of the world's cities. Every day, cars, bikes and mass transit drop off thousands of workers at their office where they make their way to sit at their desk. Going to the office gives us a purpose. It gives us a routine. It allows for human contact. But as you look at the reality of office life objectively it is easy to see that much is driven by habit rather than need.

Initially lockdown didn't really confront many of the issues and shortcomings of office life. For many it felt like an unreal break, almost like an extended holiday. Yes, it turned everything upside down but the assumption was that things would return to normal and that the primacy of the office was the default position.

But the extended lockdown started to challenge that assumption and brought many issues to the fore. Leaders found themselves less able to rely on their traditional levers of authority and action. They had to reappraise timescales and began to realise that teams, functions, reporting lines and normal ways of doing business weren't necessarily as effective as they should be. Decades of incremental change had left the shibboleths of office life largely unchecked.

The lockdown showed us an alternative. It gave many people the taste of other options. It shone a light on the whole issues of offices: how much do we need them, do we all need to be there at the same time and what are they actually for.

Why is any of this important? It's because this is the reality for the people you're leading. You may focus on the strategy, operations and managing day-to-day issues, but many of the people you lead are often more concerned with how they work, why they work, where they work and whether the trains will be running on time to get them home.

Let's face it, much of office life was pretty poor. All those "great place to work" surveys, bean bags and free fruit didn't really fool us. For many, work was a paycheck, a chance to be occupied rather than kick their heels and an opportunity to get out of the house.

> The sooner that leaders recognise the reality of the nature of work, the better they'll adapt to leading in the new, more fluid and more flexible environment

Now is the time to rethink, relearn, renew. It is time to repurpose leadership style and to create a work process and culture that is less fixed on a physical office and is more in tune with our flexible times.

At its most basic level, what people want from their leaders is the "What, the How and the Why". The truth is that most leaders tend to specialise in the "What". They provide big picture visions and set the strategic frameworks. They then position themselves as the decision-maker in chief, focusing on execution. Most still see their role as leading by example from the front.

The "How" of work is delegated to their direct reports, line managers and specialists. They're the people who actually know how to do things and how to make things happen. Leaders think that they provide the "Why" in their employees' lives, but actually purpose in itself is not enough.

In truth, leaders effectively used rewards to provide the "Why". Salaries, bonuses, fruit and gym passes: they are the "Why".

Today's leaders need to recognise that everyone went through a trauma with the pandemic. On the surface it may not seem like it, but deep down, many people were profoundly unsettled by the experience.

The post-lockdown leader

Leaders need to help rekindle a passion for work while at the same time understanding that many of life's boundaries have been broken. It's clear that the prolonged physical absence from one's work community has impacted how people work. It's been tough to establish the right levels of connectivity and relearn how to collaborate effectively.

A new style of leadership is required. No one will have the luxury of simply going back to how things were. It won't be possible to reboot and expect operations to be fully restored. The Black Swan event was there all along. Hiding in plain sight. We just chose to assume that any business interruption would be minimal, manageable and short-lived (I remember being on a crisis team during the Bird flu scare in 2007 when our biggest focus was getting stocks of Tamiflu. Changing how we managed the business was not on the agenda).

The external pressures on leaders are great. Consumer demand will change. People will shift their priorities and spending habits. Supply chains will need to be reconsidered, with pressure to become less reliant on Just in Time and more towards Just in Case. The financial implications will be immense.

Many leaders will need to develop new models for their businesses. Strategy will need to take into account all the various elements of the new environment, from operations to organisational design.

At the same time, leaders will need to build a new culture, a culture fit for purpose in this new world. They will need to offer clarity and energy. What they can't do is dip into the old leadership toolkit.

Working from home will be both a blessing and a curse. The best leaders will understand that they need to seize the opportunity. This is the chance to change things for the better. But to win in this brave new world they will need a new leadership playbook. And this is it.

3 THE NEW WORLD OF WORK – HOME SWEET HOME

Plenty of sayings and songs have been written about the home. After all, home is where the heart is. And, until recently, it had, for the majority of people, been separate from work. Lockdown changed all that. Uninvited and unexpected, work invaded the home.

This unplanned intrusion into our lives had many consequences. Some positive but many negative. Most importantly, it blurred the boundaries between work life and private life. Of course, technology made that journey first but this is different. Work has driven its tanks in and parked them in our kitchens and spare bedrooms. It is very difficult to escape work, meaning that compartmentalising our work/life balance has never been so difficult.

The reality of home working

To be effective, leaders need to understand the reality of work now for the people that they lead. For many the practicalities of working from home are formidable.

Not everyone has the right physical space, tools and personal circumstances. Some are forced to work from a kitchen table or a spare bedroom. Many have to share with partners or flatmates who are also working. Children of all ages present significant issues, from young babies and toddlers who need constant attention, to school age teenagers who require motivation, supervision and emotional support. Some share their living space with elderly relatives. Others provide help for vulnerable neighbours.

And priorities shift during the day. Not just the focus of attention, but maybe even internet bandwidth. If broadband connectivity is at a premium, then there's a trade-off between whether a work Zoom call, home schooling, job interviews or even Netflix is the most important at the time.

Not only do few people have homes that are physically set up for home working, they are not emotionally set up either. For most of us home is where we came to relax and recover from work. Work is tough, emotionally and physically. And there's the commuting. Home was for down time. And even those parents who took an extremely active role in their child's education will have now been confronted with the fact that growing up and learning, both mentally and spiritually, was happening at home. Whether we like it or not, many of us had actually outsourced key parts of our child's upbringing. But growing up is often what happens between lessons. Parental role modelling and guidance has never been more influential. And, again, because the home working scenario crept up on us unawares, many of us may have not been prepared for the changes expected of us.

Roles & identity

It is also psychologically tricky switching role midstream. We all like to think that we are the same person whatever the circumstances, that we present an authentic version of ourselves. But the truth is that we rarely do. Each circumstance requires a slightly different version of us.

Our core may be the same, but we use differing behavioural traits when dealing with toddler tantrums or homework issues than we do when hosting executive team meetings. And this is what can cause the discontinuity in people's minds.

At what point does someone stop being the senior partner in a law firm and start becoming mummy making tea for the kids. Different roles mean different mindsets. It's not easy for your team members and it's not easy for the people they live with. Some may be ok with it, but the vast majority are learning as they go along. The occasional bit of weekend or evening work may have been relatively easy to manage, but full-time, day in day out is tough. People struggle with sense of identity when things are out of alignment.

We are also tribal by nature. We often tend to identify with groups. Groups help us to belong and to make sense of what we're doing. We were on a shared journey. Being apart and working remotely can fracture that contract. Isolation is really tough.

Time

Time is another big issue that differs hugely from working together in a physical office. We may think that social media and technology had already blurred time, but that was nothing compared with full-on working from home. For each person, the day takes on its own rhythm. Weekdays and weekends seem to merge. In these circumstances, phrases like Close of Play and End of Business become meaningless. As do timescales and many deadlines. When home and work become one, who sets the priorities? Juggling around bath time and bedtime for kids, family meals, dogs that need walking, shopping that has to be done. That's all tough at the best of times, but add in bosses with deadlines and client calls and everything becomes much harder.

Global businesses add another dimension beyond time zones. Each country and region approached the lockdown in different ways. Media reporting and government actions create a different context. Restrictions and differing cultural norms mean reactions are different both physically affecting how people work and their levels of positive and negative sentiment.

Change

As a leader, you're used to change. Your business life is all about constantly improving. You've seen countless presentations that quote Heraclitus as saying that the only constant in life is change. Most people like to think that they can embrace change. But, in fact, most struggle. We're creatures of habit. We like our routines, our ways of working. Familiar surroundings and familiar faces. Change is unsettling. We don't like it when things get turned upside down.

The pace and the unexpected nature of enforced lockdown affected everybody. Nobody asked for it, nobody wanted it, and few expected it to be either as severe or in force for so long. Your teams will have been through a whole range of emotions. They will have been questioning many aspects of their work life, their home life and their relationships. There is little worse than being forced to assume roles and behaviours that were not expected, and for plans and aspirations to have been thwarted.

People react to change differently. It takes time to work things out, to try things differently. It is wrong to underestimate how traumatic the change has been for many people. And, of course, we're not just responsible for our own feelings but we take on the emotional burdens for our family and partners as well.

Perhaps now business leaders can understand why so few change programmes actually produce results. Most people tend to be change averse. And people don't like having change thrust on them.

People are more likely to embrace change when they're the agents of change and they're more likely to resist when they're objects of change

Anxiety & Stress

Lockdown led to high levels of stress. It was inevitable with so much uncertainty. We were worried about our jobs and our security and we were worried about getting ill. We were worried about the effect on our children. We were separated from our parents and other family members. We were questioning: why now, what else, how long will it last? Unknowable and unanswerable questions. We craved certainty where there could be none. We were full of emotions. And all those toxic emotions came together in one big emotion that everyone suffered from. It had a name. It was called fear.

That sense of fear may have lessened over time but it's going to take a long time for people to get to a place where they feel comfortable again. Fear may have changed into either anger or frustration. Few were in a place of calm acceptance.

Remember: no one had any experience of anything like lockdown before. No one was physically or mentally prepared. We each had to make our own journey, each reacting in our own way

There was never going to be one right answer and no one-size-fits-all approach. We all had to find our own way to manage the many conflicting demands.

And in times of great uncertainty people crave true leadership. They don't want to be told that all will be well when they know that no one can promise that. They just want the truth. They want honesty. Practical and pragmatic honesty from a strong leader who doesn't panic.

Leaders need to recognise all these practical issues, needs and emotions in their teams. They need to face up to the reality that everyone has gone through. Lockdown and working from home was not normal. True leaders get it. And they get that in order to lead others they must first lead themselves.

4 LEADING YOURSELF

First lead yourself

> As they always say during airline safety briefings: fix your own oxygen mask before helping others

Before you can lead your teams in this new reality, you first need to lead yourself. Focus on yourself and get your house in order. You have to face the same issues, the same conflicts, fears and emotions. You need to build a resilience that you may not have had before.

You cannot lead 24/7 at home.

- It's not good for you.
- It's not good for your teams
- And it's not good for those you live with

There has never been a more important moment for you to invest in yourself. The impact of the changes that your business is facing will challenge you both physically and mentally. You need to do more than recognise this fact. You need to actively confront it. You need to think about what new skills you will need and what existing behaviours and attitudes are no longer relevant. Significant aspects of your normal routine may have to be altered in order for you to continue to be an effective leader.

Now is the perfect time to learn some new good habits and to ditch some old bad habits

People are looking to you. You are having to make complex and challenging decisions in an ever-changing environment. Your teams need you to be at the top of your game. You need to balance honesty and telling it how it is, with a sense of optimism. Doom and gloom are dispiriting. But now is not the time for a Chief Entertainment Officer. Realism and pragmatism are what's wanted now. You need to treat people like adults while recognising their vulnerability. It's a hugely difficult balancing act.

Your team are looking to you for answers despite knowing that you don't have them all. Your team are looking to you for certainty despite knowing that it's not something that you can offer. And your team are looking for a calm head in a crisis, and whether you can offer that is entirely down to you.

The most likely scenario is that society will be living with elements of a lockdown for the foreseeable future. While elements will revert to something like near normal, work and life will be forever changed by the experience. This means that your leadership style will have to adapt to incorporate many new ways of thinking and leading. Rethink, relearn and renew. What worked before won't necessarily work in the future. Things have changed: emotionally, physically, behaviourally and attitudinally. We've all been shaped by the experience.

Everyone panicked at the start of the lockdown. But leaders can't remain in panic mode. Cool heads and calm thinking are required. Because we're in it for the long term. It represents a fundamental shift in our thinking and behaviour. And running at full pace is not going to help. It's unsustainable. You need to pace yourself physically and mentally.

Do you remember your first bicycle? It probably had stabilisers but it didn't have any gears. Our little legs used to race around at top speed. And then our next bike came with actual gears. And when we learnt how they worked we realised that we could go faster with less effort. If we slowed down, we could actually be more effective. It's a big lesson for life. The calmer we are, the more effective we can be. And that's what your teams want from you, especially now.

Being calm starts with our core. Who we are and what we're all about. It's the true centre of our being.

Now is the time to ask yourself some fundamental questions:

- Who do I want to be at this stage?
- How should I act?
- How do I want to be judged?
- Am I ready to take on this challenge?
- What in my past has prepared me to lead at this difficult time?
- What strengths do I need to draw upon?

These are all important questions. And they are not easy. Blindly setting out on a journey without pausing to reflect is not advisable. It really is worth taking some time to be clear with yourself about your own character and how you lead yourself.

Which brings us back to the core. The core of who we are. The fundamentals of our personality. Our purpose and our values. Our beliefs and our ambitions. We've invested a great deal in our foundations and they are what give us the strength to act and lead in difficult and trying circumstances.

Pretty much all physical activity is built around a strong core. It allows us to carry out our key role and to be flexible enough to adapt to new challenges.

So, the starting point is to reaffirm your key purpose. If you can't correlate your "Why" with the new reality, then you're not going to be the right person to lead. If your heart isn't in it, then your mind won't be either. And your teams will see through you pretty quickly.

It is very likely that you're going to have to make some adaptations to your purpose. It may need to be tweaked. You may have to roll some goals in or extend time horizons. But your key foundations should be pretty similar.

Let's face it, you're going to be asking more from the people you lead. They're going to have to find new ways to face what's thrown at them. They're going to have to find hidden strengths and learn new tools. So it's likely that you're going to have to as well.

Start by doing a mental inventory of how well equipped you are to lead in the new environment. Now is the time to be the change you want to see.

It takes a while for leaders to realise that, when it comes to behaviours, people don't do what they're told. They do what they see. If, as a leader, you say one thing and do another, then guess what, people just follow your lead. And this is just as true in a virtual environment. Your leadership style – how you act and behave – sets the tone. You have to exhibit, live, breathe the behavioural traits that you want others to follow. For instance, if you take time in the middle of the day to go for a walk, then you give others permission to do the same.

Sort out your physical workspace

The likelihood is that at your permanent office you have a space that you call your own. Even if you're unlucky enough to be in an open plan environment, the chances are that you have your own desk.

And most of you will have a desk that works for you. It will be the right size for your needs and, importantly, the right height. You'll have the light you need, the technology and equipment, and you'll be sitting on a chair that supports your back and is adjustable. We take many of these things for granted. In fact, it's only when we don't have them that we realise just how important they are. Bad backs and eye strain are common among enforced homeworkers.

Twenty years' ago home working was first introduced at the company I was working for. Even though, for me, it would never be for more than once or twice a month, I was given a workplace assessment.

Someone came to the house, fitted up the desk and chair, assessed the lighting, and cabled up computers and printers. Anyone who is going to spend time working at home needs to do what they can to make the physical environment fit for purpose.

If you can, set up a permanent workstation. Ideally, it should be away from the family. If you don't have an office set up with a closed door, then commandeer a spare bedroom. Best still is to build an office in a shed in the garden. It may sound odd but there is much to be said from a physical separation between work and home, even if it's only a walk to the end of the garden.

Physical separation is also helpful for family members and partners. Work/life balance is not all about sharing the kitchen table. Many people can come to resent the constant intrusion. You may also want to think about what you wear. I know people who change at the end of their working day. It's a bit like taking off a uniform. Taking a shower and putting on a fresh set of clothes can signal the end of the (home) office work and the start of family time. It's not a question of wearing a collar and tie one minute and a T-shirt the next. But it can help to act as a visual cue to family members: the boss has finished and Mum's back.

Check in on your mental state

As we've said, the effect of the lockdown and the implications of long-term, enforced homeworking is stressful. The context in which people are having to work obviously differs but the impact of so many changes added to economic and health concerns can cause major anxiety. Having the burden of leadership exacerbates the issue. Not only are you trying to scenario plan and lead, but you have the responsibility of your team's livelihoods. Leadership is never easy. Leading from home makes it harder.

And when you don't have your teams around you, it makes it more difficult to recognise your own issues with stress. Many leaders struggle to see the signs of burnout. Constantly working under pressure, with uncertain limitations on work and down time, create breeding grounds for stress. And this is at a time when your teams require you to be operating at peak performance. Never has it been more important to have a healthy mind and a healthy body.

A calm mind is an emotionally and rationally balanced mind. It is a mind that can keep things in perspective and one that doesn't jump to conclusions. A calm mind can balance the lessons of the past with the potential scenarios of the future. A calm mind can focus on what's important while holding multiple ideas.

But a calm mind doesn't always come naturally. Like most things, it takes practice. And the more you practise, the better you get.

So, if you want to be an effective leader in these times of increased stress and uncertainty, then build in mental exercises to help you stay calm.

There are plenty of books about meditation, mindfulness and breathing. And there are plenty of academic studies that point to the physiological benefits. Nearly all techniques start with the breath.

Even when I coach leaders on communicating, I cover breathing. Public speaking can be nerve-racking for some. So, I tell them that before they start and between paragraphs to simply Pause, Breathe and Smile. And it works. Stress and tension simply evaporate.

You'll find what's right for you. It may be an early morning meditation session or a post-lunch mindfulness exercise. For me, I simply try to focus on my breathing as often as I can. And once an hour or so I relax my shoulders, take a deep breath and hold for five seconds. Then breathe out and hold for another five seconds. And repeat four or five times.

Stretching is good as well. Many people find that when working from home they actually move around less. In an office environment they may get up to go and see someone, pick up some printing and generally move around a lot.

Working from a home desk seems to make people more static. They spend hours hunched over their laptops. Don't make this mistake. Take frequent time out to stretch and move around.

Exercise. Seriously, you just need to do it

You don't need to be a corporate athlete with an Iron Man course in your garden but you do need to be disciplined about exercise. In fact, this is one of the few topics in this book that does not need to be laboured. Most leaders have already got this point.

Spend time in nature

One interesting observation that I've heard from many people is that the lockdown gave them the opportunity to be more aware of the changing seasons. For many people when it started the trees were leafless and the ground was bare. And people said that they seemed to take more notice of Spring bursting into life than they can remember doing before. Perhaps it was because they'd slowed down. Maybe it was because they spent more time around their home. And it could also be because they wanted to find signs of hope; that things would get better. Whatever it was, there is much to be gained from giving yourself the chance to spend time in nature.

Take the time to be grateful and thankful. Listen with your ears and look with your eyes. Whatever the circumstances of your home working environment, there will be birdsong to hear and flowers to enjoy. It really is incredibly important to feel grounded and recognise that, despite the situation and uncertainty, the sun will still set in the evening and rise in the morning.

We all have our own ways of relaxing. I used to find mine through exertion and activity. That's still important. But the fact is that running to relax can sometimes be a displacement exercise. You can run but you can't hide from yourself. Relaxing is all about feeling comfortable in the moment. And that's important when confined to working from home for extended periods.

> The last thing that you want to do is to take work issues to the family. Subconsciously offloading work stress on family members happens more than you think. Relaxing and switching off are key to compartmentalising

For leaders, who have allowed work to dominate their lives and their relationships, it can take time to relearn how to switch off. When we were kids our parents would get angry when we said we were bored. How could we be bored when there was so much we could be doing. Actually, sometimes we do too much. There's a lot to be said for mooching around. Just enjoying being with the family and loving the little things. Read books, share silly stuff, do family jigsaws and Zoom quizzes. Few people go to their graves wishing that they'd spent more time at the office. Well, now is your chance to make the most of it.

Finally, it's also good to learn something new. Or, indeed, to pick up something again. Maybe that guitar.

Refashion your attitudes

Ideas about the most effective approach to leadership have undergone many changes in the past decades. But pretty much everyone would argue that going around barking orders and shouting at subordinates is not the best way to get results. Encouraging others, building teams and projecting visions require softer and subtler approaches to leadership.

It is often said that TV changes how people look. The screen tends to make large people look larger and small people look smaller. It seems to accentuate differences. Minor insignificances assume greater impact. The same can be said for working from home. Perhaps it's the distance. Being physically apart makes it more difficult to pick up on visual or non-verbal cues. Perhaps it's the emotional strain of extended isolation and lockdown.

It took a while to realise that some methods of communication were not suitable for the messages we were trying to convey. Many of us learnt the hard way that irony is often lost on email and that tweets can be taken out of context. The same is true of leading from home. We have to recognise that everything about it is different and that it requires a different attitude to leadership.

The biggest attitudinal skill that leaders leading from home need to develop is empathy. You may feel that you were pretty good before but however good you were, you need to dial it up. Your empathy needs to be transmitted over a greater distance and so it needs more power behind it.

Your teams are making big sacrifices. They're losing out on things they were looking forward to, they're making big compromises and they're working for you in what can often be very difficult and challenging circumstances. It is not enough for you to say that you understand their plight. Compassion and empathy require you to dig deep.

One attitudinal attribute that can help enormously with empathy is active listening. This is a real skill and takes time to develop. It requires you to not only pay attention to what is, and what is not, being said but you also need to demonstrate that you're listening. You need to give feedback. You need to find the appropriate ways to respond. And you need to make sure that you are being non-judgemental. That's a lot to ask in a face-to-face environment. So, think how much more you need to do if you're speaking with someone sitting at their kitchen table across an unstable internet connection.

One way that helps with both empathy and active listening is to admit to being vulnerable. It's not something that leaders often do. For many, they put on the suit of permanent invincibility, their Superman cape. But not everyone is fooled. They know that leaders are human beings and that they suffer the same vicissitudes as everyone else. It's just that leaders rarely show their emotions.

Accepting vulnerability is a sign of strength not a sign of weakness. It is an acknowledgement that we're all in the same boat, facing similar issues and similar challenges

People want to be led by honest leaders. Leaders who are not afraid to call it as it is. It's tough. It's difficult. Telling the truth and giving expression to the fear is a way of confronting it. Sincerity has its own rewards. People like to be led by humans and not emotionless robots. And if they feel that you really are like one of them, then you'll find that they give more back.

As we said, offloading work issues and stress on family members and partners is not a good thing. There is a massive difference between sharing and offloading. The former is a way of building rapport and understanding.

The latter is simply passing off worries and concerns. You may feel lighter by offloading but the other person is merely weighed down by your problems.

And while we're on the subject, where do you go to for advice? We all need someone with whom we can talk things through. As we find in coaching and many talking therapies, a feeling or an understanding doesn't actually exist until it's been verbalised. Only when we say something out loud do we give voice to an issue or problem. Talking is good.

At the office you may have a team around you. Trusted advisors, friends, people who come to you and to whom you go to chat things through. Perhaps they just sit and listen. Perhaps they give you feedback, opening up an insight into some part of your behaviour of which you weren't aware. We all need that opportunity in our lives.

But what about at home? It's much more difficult to find the opportunity to chat informally. Calling people at home just to chew the cud seems improper. It feels intrusive to invite yourself around virtually for a chat. Spontaneous water cooler moments don't exist. Serendipitous meetings in coffee shops are less likely. So, you're going to have to be more formal. Talking is important which means that you are going to have to be much more structured. Build sessions with your coach or advisor into your weekly routine. Uncertain times and extended periods away from the office make sharing your thoughts and concerns with a professional more important than ever.

Loneliness among senior executives has always been a big issue. Despite having so many people who are, in theory at least, at their disposal, leaders often rely on increasingly small numbers of trusted people. Curiously, it is also possible to feel lonely at home. You may be surrounded by your family but because you feel unable or unwilling to share your work issues with them there is a tendency to turn inwards.

This can lead to a sense of loneliness. Literally, you have no one to turn to. And that's why it is so important to find a third-party professional with whom to share.

As we've said, working from home exacerbates and magnifies all emotional responses. You need to find someone to check in with.

All of this is seriously important because if you don't focus on your mental attitudes and develop real resilience, then others won't either. Leaders are role models. They set the standards and the expectations. They have to live and breathe the business values. Your people mirror the behaviours that come down from the top. And even if they don't see you around, your leadership style still percolates through the organisation.□

5 LEADING YOUR TEAM

Trust

Leadership minus trust equals authority

Leadership without trust is merely authority. Telling people what to do is not leadership. Issuing orders merely reflects a hierarchy of status. Being higher up the chain of command gives you the right to tell those below you what to do.

Many international surveys have shown levels of trust across society to be on a downward trend. Figures of authority seem to be held in far lower regard than their predecessors holding similar positions in the past. Some say that it is because society now has much higher expectations of standards of behaviour. Others point to the greater levels of scrutiny available, for instance, thanks to the ubiquity of smart phones and social media bad behaviour can be captured and shared quickly.

Whatever the various reasons, trust in many professions is generally lower than it was. And business leaders are no exception.

Employees, who as members of society, hold business leaders generally in low regard, don't suddenly change their mind when they come to work. They hold equally sceptical thoughts about the leaders of the organisations that they work for. The starting point is low. They need to be convinced. They need reasons to trust their leaders. Trust is not automatically assumed or given.

To be a true leader requires being trusted.

But many people get confused by the concept of trust. They see it as an input. They do things in order to gain trust.

Trust is actually an outcome. You can't make people trust you and you cannot tell them to trust you. Trust has to be earned. You need to do things consistently over time, acting with fairness and equality. Your actions, in total, should result in you gaining a reputation for being honest, truthful, reliable and consistent. Taken together, those attributes, given to you by others, result in trust.

And if you can be trusted, people will follow. And if they follow, together you can achieve your goals.

Communications

As we've already said, you can't just tell people what to do. It's something we all know in theory, but somehow we forget it. Especially in the workplace. It stands out most with children. Despite telling them what to do, those pesky kids simply end up imitating and copying what their parents do. It's infuriating when children point out that you've got your feet on the couch, or you didn't use a handkerchief, or that you were also talking with your mouth full. Their eagle eyes are always on the lookout for parental fallibility.

Many business leaders forget this simple lesson. They often behave as if the rules they make don't apply to them. Cost cutting is a prime example.

Every time a new savings initiative is launched employees never fail to notice that the exhortations of senior management to save every dime or penny rarely includes first-class travel for the executive suite. Employees notice if there's one rule for them and another rule for their leaders. And then leaders wonder why change initiatives don't work.

Communications is a poor proxy for behaviour

So before worrying about how to communicate from home, first think about your own actions and behaviours. Everything that you want to communicate, every new initiative and every new approach needs first to be a reflection of your own behaviour. Do it first, then talk about it.

Communicating effectively

You've probably heard that the robots are coming for your job. They've already replaced many blue-collar jobs. Just think how few people there are on your shop floors. In fact, whenever you take visitors around a manufacturing plant, the first thing they ask is where all the people are. So are the robots going to replace CEOs? It's worth thinking how much of a leader's job could be outsourced to an artificial CEO. Certainly, much financial decision-making could be and much of the result may well be far better. In fact, as with many other situations, it's the hard skills that are replaced first. What's left tend to be the soft skills. The human touch as we used to call it. And yet, business schools spend much of their time emphasising the hard skills.

One of the biggest so-called soft skills is communication. And yet for so many leaders it is hardly a core competence. But without communication skills it is not possible to build coalitions, to gain trust or to establish visions.

Without communication there can be no leadership

As with every other aspect of leadership, the lockdown has affected every aspect of communication. Leaders need to radically rethink not only the "How" of their communications, but the "What, Why, and When". The channels and strategy that you employed when most of your teams were in the office need rethinking. They may have worked in the past, but they're unlikely to be effective in the current circumstances.

One of the biggest assumptions about working from home was that it would free up time. The opposite, it seems, is true. Many people report that they are working harder than before. Maybe it's the concentrated effort that makes it seem that way. Maybe it just seems more relentless. Whatever it is, working from home is hard. And when times are hard, the last thing that people want is interruptions.

So, the first thing that you need to be clear about is what is your communication for? What is your message intended to achieve? Just because you are the leader, it does not give you the right to appear in everyone's inbox or on their screen.

Before you send your leadership communication, ask yourself some questions:

- Is it for information?
- Is it for action?
- Is it for action now?
- Is it for everyone?
- Does it have to come from you?
- Does it have to come out now?
- How important is it relative to all the other messages people are receiving?
- Is it intended to change how your teams act or think?
- Is it for public consumption or internal only?

The answers to these questions should determine if it's necessary, if it needs to be right now and what is the most appropriate channel.

Information overload hasn't gone away with working from home. In some cases, it seems to have got worse. That's why it is important for your employees to know where your communication sits in their hierarchy of needs. Some businesses have introduced fairly strict rules that flag up what sort of communication it is. For instance, red-flagged emails for urgent and important action updates, green flags for non-time sensitive information updates and weekly intranet bulletins for leadership updates.

Others flag up whether a communication is for information only or for action. This sort of categorisation could help your employees manage their information flow.

The point of this flagging of importance is that just because it comes from the leader doesn't mean that it automatically has to go to the top of the pile.

Leaders have to earn the right to be listened to. If you have nothing of interest to say, or you choose the wrong time or the wrong medium, then your employees will simply switch off.

It is important to keep communications regular and consistent and leaders need to be visible, but don't dilute your message by continually popping up uninvited

Some marketeers will talk about the difference between pull and push communication. In the past, advertising was pushed out to captive audiences who sat at home during commercial breaks and received whatever information you wanted to promote about your brand at a time of choosing.

Over time, much brand communication has switched to pull communications, whereby the consumer has the ability to choose not just when they receive your messages, but also how. And rather than simply receive the messages that you may have wanted to promulgate, they may want to have more of a conversation. These trends are as relevant and valid internally with your employees as they are externally with your customers.

Leadership communications also needs to be both clear and consistent. Establishing a rhythm is always important but never more so than when the business is operating out of people's homes. As we mentioned previously, uncertain times breed fear. And so being consistent in how you approach both content and timing can help manage expectations.

Video calls

One of the biggest technological advances in recent years is that video calls are now so well embedded. Everyone, including elderly relatives on family quiz nights, seem to have got the hang of them. They're great for seeing people, keeping in touch and making people feel part of a team. Many leaders use them a great deal.

But you should use video calls sparingly. The fact is that they're not good for every type of call or communication.

Video calls are tiring. We're programmed to maintain eye contact and on a video call we have to do it much more than we would in a physical meeting. We also have to try to work out when to speak. Because picture and sound are sent separately there will always be a gap (sometimes tiny, sometimes extended) between the voice and the picture. As humans, whenever we see or sense a gap, we tend to jump in. And this can mean that you get lots of people trying to speak at the same time.

And video calls can be intrusive. It's a bit like your neighbours popping round. The first time it's nice, the second time it's good, but if they keep inviting themselves over it can seem a bit unwelcome. And that's the same with video calls.

> With video calls you are basically inviting yourself into someone's home. And not everyone is comfortable with that. Don't pop around too often

As we've already covered, not everyone has a home office separate from the rest of the house. Some are working from a bedroom. Some are using the dressing table as their desk. Some are in cramped surroundings with little storage space. Many are sharing workspaces with other household members and some are having to ration broadband band width.

Video calls bring into sharp focus that working from home means working around other priorities. Babies may need feeding and pets may need attention. And just because your call takes place during "office hours" why should you take precedence for attention over a child who wants help with their homework or over a family lunch.

And there are people who are concerned about how they look. Midway through the lockdown people seemed to become very conscious about their hair. Maybe it was too long, maybe too many grey hairs were starting to stick out. Appearances matter and video calls mean that there is nowhere to hide.

One suggestion is to start some meetings with video as a way of saying hello and catching up and then switching the camera off until the end.

Video calls are good for many forms of meeting and communications. They can work well for Town Halls but, as with all similar meetings, they work best with a host who can chair the meeting and manage Q&A sessions.

For many broadcast video messages, it is often best to record them so that employees can choose to watch them when it is convenient for them. It means that, again, leadership messages take their place in the hierarchy of work, dog walking, children's baths, family mealtimes and all the other things that actually have to take place in order for a family to function.

Don't ask or expect your employees to drop everything simply to watch your update at a time of your choosing

So, before you ask your teams to switch their cameras on, ask yourself whether it really is necessary for it to be a video call or are you just being nosy.

Communications style

As the saying goes, it's not what you say, it's the way that you say it. At times like these it can be easy to ruin a good message by getting the tone or the delivery wrong. Tempting though it is to be the corporate cheerleader, always looking on the bright side, what your people actually want is honesty and reliable information. So, think about how you communicate. Aim to share and not tell.

And tell stories and paint pictures. Use any data as the foundation and to illustrate your story rather than using it as the message itself.

> Facts and data points can never get the same emotional response as a good narrative

Coaching

At the start of the crisis your leadership style was tested. Things happened very fast. There was a lack of solid information but no lack of various different stakeholders wanting decisions and answers. Now you've had time to shift gears. You're pedalling more efficiently.

> Now is the time to change your leadership style from decision-maker in chief to coach

Rushing around giving orders and making decisions is not what's needed now. Your leadership style needs to shift. It needs to be more inclusive. Your role now is to create the environment in which decisions can be taken. It's more than delegating. And it's more than giving permission. It's about a new form of leading. It's about coaching.

At its most basic you'd say that a boss tells you what to do. An advisor tells you how to do it. A mentor tells you what they would have done at your age. But a coach asks questions.

Coaching helps people find the answers themselves. It helps them look inside for solutions. It helps them to grow and to be independent rather than dependent on their boss.

> Coaching is a much more effective management approach. It builds long-term, sustainable improvements in performance and behaviours. It creates self-awareness and develops resilience. At times of uncertainty and in difficult circumstances it is invaluable

Listening

One of the most difficult skills to master as a coach is that of listening. It is odd, because everyone thinks of themselves as a good listener and most people don't think there's an issue. But actually it's very hard to listen well. In the same way that many people look without properly seeing, some hear without properly listening. Properly listening to what is being said, what's not being said, and the pauses between.

Think about the many meetings you've been in. How many people really listen? In many cases, it's more a case of everyone taking it in turns to be silent until it is their turn to speak. They don't listen, they think about and mentally rehearse what they're going to say. They make notes, they check their phones. And maybe they'll pick up on one or two points.

Active listening is tough. Active, non-judgemental listening is even tougher. It's hard to put yourself in a position where you are really concentrating on what is being said, and what is being communicated to you, rather than thinking about how you feel about what you're hearing. Often, people tell you things because they're looking to you to make a decision. And so you'll often find yourself thinking more about how you are going to react rather than fully giving yourself over to what's being discussed.

Another aspect of listening is that it is about you, as the leader, making space for other people. Many leaders, unfortunately, communicate and talk too much. Sometimes a sense of importance can go to their heads. They end up talking too much and too often. They spend most of their time on project mode. And when they do pause, it's not to allow others to contribute, it's so that they can reload.

But working remotely has changed all that.

> Leaders need to be much more aware of truly listening to what's being said. If they talk too much, then they won't be able to pick up what's really being transmitted

Asking good questions

Another good coaching skill that is even more essential for leaders when leading remote teams is asking good questions. In fact, asking good questions is an art form. The intervention of a well-timed question can elicit more information than anything else.

A good question should make someone pause and inwardly reflect. A good question should be open and it should be neutral. It should not be judgemental. A good question should not lead the listener to wonder why you've asked that question, it should make them reflect.

Why do you say that, why do you think that, is that all there is to it, what else, if you knew the answer what would it be? These are all great questions designed to bring out and uncover the real issues.

Because when you're leading remotely, you can't do everyone else's job. If your corporate culture is that things are upwardly delegated, then you are going to collapse under the weight of making all the decisions. And if you are always the ultimate sign-off then no-one will ever learn to take responsibility for themselves and all attempts to delegate will fail.

Good coaching not only helps unlock your team's potential, but it can really help to build their self-awareness and self-belief and lead to them taking far greater responsibility for their actions. For leaders, it represents a shift from a management style towards a more empowered, open and transformed culture.

Humour

Another attitude that might need reappraising is your approach to humour. Some people think that work is too serious for humour. Others think that the only way to make sense of work is to laugh at it. The lockdown crisis certainly showed the power of humour. For many, joking was the best way to deal with it. Certainly, the outpouring of creativity that went into viral videos helped to lighten the mood. Of course, the lockdown has been devastating. And, of course, there's nothing funny about having to let people go. However, sometimes finding amusement and sharing it is the right thing to do. Humour brings people together. Levity is an important part of our humanity. The UK's Royal Marines lists humour as one of its leadership attributes on the basis that when you're in the worst of all situations, then making light of it is a survival technique. After all, worse things happen at sea.

Change how you work

Now is a good time to reflect on better ways to work. Too many aspects of work have evolved over time. Remember Parkinson's Law? He very astutely said that "work expands so as to fill the time available for its completion". Likewise, we all know what happens when there's a restructuring at work. Roles and people get made redundant. But what about the work? Often it gets shared out among those left. Rarely do we stop to question what is really needed. We build on legacy systems and operations.

And that's because too often in business we tend to value input over outcome. Input is doing lots of stuff. It's being busy. It's being indispensable. Input is tackling one task after another, going to meetings, producing power-point slides, answering emails and making calls.

Output is something else entirely. Output is making a commercial, holding a conference, launching a new product. Output is what many people get measured by, incentivised by and rewarded by. Output really gets you noticed.

But output isn't what work is really about. What we should all be striving towards is outcome. Making a difference, shifting the needle. Outcome means changing things for the better. Increasing sales, shifting reputation and making a difference. Yet too many management tasks focus more on the process than the outcome.

> When looking to change operations, leaders often start at the beginning with input rather than at the end with outcome

Now is the time to change the way you look at your business. Don't look incrementally. Start by being really clear about where you are now. Understand your own strengths and weaknesses and those of your competitors. Understand the market and all the various dynamics. Then decide where you want to be. Your future, desired, state. And then work backwards, setting timeframes and milestones.

It is revealing how many people plan incrementally. Of course, it can be hugely difficult to think ahead, especially with so much disruption and uncertainty in the market. But unless you constantly take a long view and then work backwards you will be cursed with building on legacy systems and legacy thinking. You need to continually challenge yourself and your business. You need new thinking, new approaches and new attitudes. As they say, what got you here won't necessarily get you there.

And it's true of your organisational design. Traditional structures can be an asset in times of stability but a liability in times of change. Few roles these days need to be 100% specialist. Most of us need to use multiple skills to achieve our goals. And to do our jobs best we need to collaborate and cooperate with others outside our narrow functional reporting lines.

As a leader you need to encourage curiosity, collaboration, co-creation. And not just encourage these behaviours, you need to showcase them and let others follow your example.

Don't rely on the same people and the same small teams that you've always done. Bring new people and new thinking into your leadership orbit. If you want to encourage self-forming and self-managing teams, then you must lead the way.

Allow your teams to find the right answers themselves. Ask different questions rather than continuing to manage your business the same old way: divisions, countries, product groups, job grades. Just because you've always done it that way doesn't mean you can't find a better way.

Set an example by challenging yourself. The world has changed and perhaps the biggest barrier to your business changing is that you continue to see it through an old lens.

Business issues will be solved by allowing your people to find solutions. Keeping people and their roles stuck in silos will hinder the process.

You should see your role as mandating the "What" but not the "How"

Let your people find the best routes. And don't be surprised if they find better solutions than you expected. It's amazing what a bit of creative thinking can bring to old problems.

In a period of resetting and rethinking, now is a good time to take a look in the mirror. You also will have picked up some bad habits. You also could learn some new tricks. Be honest with yourself. Are you actually good at everything?

Over time leaders often take on too much. They think that they have to be involved in every decision and that nothing can happen without their knowledge. Perhaps it's time to actually stop doing things. Just get out of the way.

Don't just do something, stand there

Speed is a big factor. Post lockdown, many struggling businesses will be playing catch-up: catch-up with their customers, suppliers and competitors. So be realistic about what you can achieve. Voltaire said that perfect is the enemy of good. Robert Alexander-Watson, one of the early pioneers of radar during World War II, said: "Give them the third best to go on with; the second best comes too late; and the best never comes." Find your own answer to the 80/20 conundrum but be realistic. These are unusual times and there will never be a perfect answer to a solution. So, try to resist the urge to gold-plate everything.

Office hours

I was always quite taken with those characters in early 20th-century novels who would stroll into the office around 10am, go out for lunch at midday, and then leave for home at 4pm. And they had the luxury of leaving work behind with no smart phone constantly receiving emails and messages. In those days it was rare for work to impinge on home life. How different business life was before lockdown. Long days in the office and then the emails followed you home. No rest for the wicked.

Of course, the idea of business hours has some merit. But many businesses operate 24 hours a day. It's just the people that come and go. Global corporations, of course, operate across multiple time zones, bringing real issues for those leading multi-country teams.

But now many of your teams are working from home. And this brings a whole new dimension to how you manage their time. And it also brings to the fore how you manage your own time.

Some businesses used to be very clear about working hours. They didn't allow their employees to do anything that was not 100% work-related while in the office. Even recently, many businesses wouldn't allow work computers to be used for home shopping. Personal phone calls were discouraged and private social media usage frowned upon. What people do in their own time is up to them, they used to say, but while they're in the office they're being paid to work.

Does that contract still work? If your teams are working from home, does it mean that between office hours of, say, 9am to 5pm they work only for you? It seems both highly improbable and highly impractical. But what sort of flexibility should you allow?

How can you know if some are not pulling their weight? Or, on the other hand, how can you be sure that others aren't working too hard?

The issue of the work/life balance is serious. It is now hugely important for everyone to be clear when they're working and when they're not. No one can be always on. No one can work 24/7. It's not healthy and it's not good for the people you live with. And babies don't only need feeding and attention before 9am and after 5pm. And the same goes for the rest of the family, including pets.

And as lockdown was extended, many organisations required staff to take some of their holiday. It may have been a sensible way to ensure that, when restrictions were relaxed, there wasn't a problem with everyone wanting to take a Summer break at the same time.

But the effect has been for employees to be in lockdown at home with no way of properly relaxing. Holidays and vacations are hugely important and necessary opportunities to recharge. But if there is literally no difference between working and not working then the mind will not settle. Stress and anxiety have fewer opportunities for release.

There is also an issue for employees who were furloughed. Not only did they have the fear of never returning to work but they were also stuck at home and not allowed to work.

Mental health has never been more tested in the work environment than it has been by transferring work to the home. Of course, many people worked at home before, but those that did may not have had to share the experience with other family members or flatmates and also take on the burden of responsibility, for instance, of full-time childcare.

This issue is not an easy one to crack. But as with pretty much everything, it starts with you. Your behaviour and your attitudes colour the whole debate.

Start by thinking how you'd like to be managed by you. Would you trust yourself to get the balance right?

- Recognise that many of the concepts traditionally associated with the office are now redundant. There can be no end of business or close of play when working from home, so don't make such demands.
- Recognise that you may pay the wages but you cannot dictate every aspect of someone's home work life.
- Recognise that asking and expecting someone to carry on working for you from their own kitchen table is a real imposition. And it's not just an imposition on your employee but also on their family members and flatmates.

Your teams have made a real sacrifice. Make a compromise. Give them the latitude to work out the best way for them to balance their competing demands. Let them work the hours that suit them. Let them take time during the day for family meals or school work or dog walking. It's up to you to be flexible and realistic. Work with them to find a mature, sensible approach to managing work and workflow.

The more you give, the more you'll get back

But, as we've said before, it all starts with your attitude and your behaviour. Why not check in with your family members and ask them if you're getting the work/home balance right. They know you best and you might be surprised how they rank you.

Ethical leadership

One of the most striking insights that occurred to me early on in my career was the number of people who behaved one way at work and another in their private life. It wasn't a unique insight but it did colour much of my attitude to my advisory work. I saw how people who were generous, welcoming, sharing and empathetic at home and with their friends would suddenly become authoritarian, didactic, impatient and inflexible when they arrived at the office.

Work, it seemed to me, had the ability to bring out the worst in people. There were rules to follow, both written and unwritten. Deadlines had to be observed. Hierarchies and status were ruthlessly adhered to (many of you, I'm sure, have been told on numerous occasions that your boss wants to see, and check, and sometimes take credit for, any piece of work that goes up the line to your boss's boss).

Mistakes weren't tolerated, perfectionism was expected. Long hours were seen as a sign of commitment. Everyone was expected to go the extra mile and give 110%. And answer emails immediately at all hours of the day.

If someone was ill, rather than express concern, I've known bosses who take it as a personal slight. As if the person had deliberately become ill to annoy their boss. Demands and pressure create stress.

The reality is that if people behaved like this in their private lives, their partners wouldn't tolerate it and their friends would desert them. So why did so many people behave badly at work? It was a conundrum. Especially as so many leaders were at the same time talking about authenticity and purpose. It seemed that many were able to hold conflicting concepts in different mental compartments. They literally could think one thing and act another.

As a coach and consultant I've always described what I do in three sentences:

- I make complex things simple
- I humanise organisations
- And I give people the confidence to see and do things differently

The first and the last of those sentences have always been the easiest to implement. Good coaching and good consulting can prove highly effective. But the middle of the three sentences has always proved to be the most ambitious.

I start with good intentions. I try hard to get leaders to see the human in all business issues. I work on the philosophy that nearly everyone wants to make a difference and to do their best.

The answers to significant amounts of any corporate challenge already lie within its people. And that through proper engagement it is possible to rise to challenges. If you work with your employees then it is possible to make significant improvements because people tend to work with you as long as they are the agents of any change rather than the objects of that change.

But it's never been as simple as that. With all the best intentions in the world, business always seems to get in the way. Organisations are, of course, inorganic and devoid of emotion. They intrinsically don't exist. And often regardless of the leadership, they can take on their own momentum. It seems that whenever the rubber hits the road it is always people who come off second best. Employees may be an organisation's greatest asset on paper but often in reality they are not.

For years it seemed difficult for leaders to see the person rather than the worker. Leaders rarely saw their employees in a home environment – as a wife, parent, carer, volunteer – and only focused on the person that they saw at work.

Until now.

> The lockdown brought the home and all its various intertwined issues viscerally into view

Now, for even the most short-sighted of leaders, it is impossible to remain ignorant of the day-to-day challenges that their teams face. Video calls confront these issues head on. From toddlers joining meetings to poor living conditions.

And beyond the video camera, life is there out of view but ever present. Abusive relationships, difficult and anxious children, loneliness and broken homes. These issues have always been there but perhaps it was all too easy to ignore them if we encouraged our teams to leave home worries and concerns at their front door and not bring them to work.

Now we've asked them to do the opposite. We've asked them to allow work to come to them, to stay with them and to impinge on the lives of everyone they live with. There is now literally no escaping work. And this means that leaders have absolutely no excuse for not seeing the human in their employees.

Because what leaders are feeling and having to confront is exactly the same for their employees. They face daily news and current affairs dominated by pandemic updates, each day whipping up more negative sentiment. They see scared children kept apart from school friends and grandparents. Worry, it seems, drove an increase in reported sleeping difficulties.

Life was put on pause.

And everyone was affected. However big the house or small the flat, people faced similar issues and were affected in similar but different ways.

Leaders can no longer draw a distinction between work and home. Work/life balance is not either one thing or another. Working from home has brought them together. Leaders have no excuse for not humanising every element of their decision-making or how they run their business.

It's all changed.

Ethical leadership means bringing the human element to the forefront. Customers, consumers, suppliers, employees, former employees. That's who the business is run for.

6 LEADING YOUR BUSINESS – THE MULTI-STAKEHOLDER MODEL

At the beginning of lockdown, when things were both strange and bewildering, maybe speed was of the essence. There were hundreds of quick fixes that needed to done. Responses needed to be immediate. Worst-case scenarios turned out not to be the worst case after all. The ground seemed to be constantly moving. The focus was on the short term. On the immediate and the obvious.

We've now moved on. Your focus needs to be different. It needs to move towards the medium and long term for your organisation. The mega societal and technological trends that were in play before the crisis are still there. And they're accelerating. AI, automation, climate change … these, and many others, are going to significantly affect your organisation and the context in which it operates. You need to accept that you cannot influence events to the extent that you may have previously thought. There are many things that are far outside your ability to control.

Your teams are looking to you to help them make sense of the new reality. Motivating just through pay cheques and promotions is too short term in such a shifting landscape.

Of course, it is always tempting to try to offer certainty, to always have the answers. But false promises no longer cut it. Everything is now hugely more complicated. You can't behave as if nothing has changed.

You need to behave differently. Now is a time for building afresh. For renewing your mindset and your organisation. The new situation requires a new attitude. You need to think, behave and act differently

When looking at the future, it's always worth bearing in mind that no one can be certain about anything. There are far too many independent and dependent permutations and the context is always shifting. However, one thing is becoming clearer. And that's that, whatever the future looks like, it won't be the same as the past. It will be similar but it will be different.

There are two reasons why we won't be returning to a pre-Covid Utopia. The first is that we won't be able to. Even if an effective vaccine becomes widely available there will still be restrictions on travel to certain places and social distancing will have profound impacts, not just on how society operates, but also on the economic viability of some industries and services. For instance, a socially-distanced bar with 25 people which previously held around 125 people. That's a big economic difference.

The second reason why we won't return to what we had before is that we won't want to. Not all of the lockdown was a bad thing. In fact, there were many aspects that we quite enjoyed. Some things were more fun, more effective, more enjoyable and better value.

In the UK, for instance, pre-lockdown the number of people having virtual consultations with their medical practitioner was around one percent.

After a few months, the figure was around 97 percent. Obviously neither figure is the optimum one; clearly there were people having virtual consultations who would have been far better off having a face-to-face meeting. But we need to see the positives in this sort of trend.

Society generally may be starting to rethink its collective priorities. The world of work was already cracking at the seams. The contract between wealth creation and society was already under strain. Add in the mega trends of healthy doses of AI, automation, demographics, disruptive technology, political volatility and climate change, and the picture looks decidedly uncertain. Covid-19 brought with it recessions, bankruptcies and economic turmoil. The impact has been profound. Businesses will have changed, people will have changed, governments will have changed.

Indeed, many governments may have gained a taste for a greater interventionist and more directive approach. Some governments may have different priorities and may now be less trusting of big business and special interest groups. Others may start to consider a more Keynesian outlook to kick-start their economies, effectively privatising key businesses or focusing spend on sectors such as infrastructure, travel, utilities, media. Other governments and regulators may intervene more in the capital markets, perhaps limiting foreign investments and takeovers or even putting stricter control on hedge funds. They may introduce rules on dividend cover and share buybacks or supply chains, shifting the focus from Just in Time to Just in Case.

Societal moods can shift quickly. In 1945 Winston Churchill went into the UK election as a war hero. He was the man who had saved the country. He was expecting to be rewarded by a grateful people. But the mood had changed.

People wanted something new rather than to go back to exactly what they had before. That's likely to happen post-lockdown. Society may want different things. It may want a rebalance of reward in favour of key workers. Perhaps it will, for instance, be less tolerant of executive pay when so many people suffer from in-work poverty. Certainly, a medical emergency that relied on so many low paid key workers demonstrated that society is only as strong as its weakest members and that an economy serves the whole of society.

And if the context changes, then businesses will have to change. They will need to reflect many of the changing priorities and attitudes. Sustainability, climate change and diversity will become bigger priorities. The consumer is likely to expect more.

The impact of the lockdown will be profound, long-term economic turmoil. There will be stress, volatility and uncertainty across the whole values chain. Even good profitable, well-managed, innovative businesses will go under. There will be questions over "efficient" business models and high leverage may cease to be quite so attractive. Maybe specialisation will become less fashionable with a shift towards conglomerates who can spread risk. Certainly, the lockdown called into question outsourcing and offshoring.

Many businesses will face existential issues, some of which they will have no control over. How many of your customers or suppliers will continue to be around? It's so difficult to know.

Many traditional business models had already started to look strained, especially as more and more financial engineering was piled on top of them. Every time boards, often under pressure from investors and banking advisors, undertook another balance sheet, or off-balance sheet, tactic, a little bit more of the original purpose of joint stock corporations was consigned to the trash can.

One thing that definitely came under pressure was the idea of the primacy of the shareholder. Extractive capitalism, with shareholders taking more than their fair share through buybacks, has long been thought to have passed its use-by date. Studies have shown that businesses with long-term, stewardship-focused backers produce better results over time than businesses backed by short-term profit chasers.

The idea of the importance of wider stakeholders in the health of a business has moved from the fringe of business seminars to the main stage. And it's now fast becoming a majority sentiment. Employees, former employees, customers, suppliers, shareholders and the community, all have a stake in the well-being of a company.

Some of the thinking around the anti-primacy of the shareholder morphed in to the Purpose arena. Every business, in addition to ESG goals, Vision, Mission, Values, employee brand propositions and the like, had to have a Purpose. Some of the exercises behind business purpose proved to be an exercise in painting lipstick on a tiger. It was post-hoc and did little or nothing to the underlying business. In other cases, it has proved to be a useful exercise in thinking long-term.

The fact remains that having a Purpose doesn't stop you going bust. Some may say that companies with a purpose are the ones that will do best post-lockdown. That may be the case, although it is most likely that it will be a spurious correlation not a result of any causation.

The new model is likely to be based on partnerships and collaboration rather than individual purpose. The lesson on society generally from lockdown was that we are only as strong as our weakest link. The same is likely to be true in business.

Co-dependence is the new model. We can only succeed if we all succeed

The fast pace of societal and technological change means that you'll have to adapt rapidly to new challenges. That means high investment in research, equipment and training. And that means less money will be available for your shareholders to extract.

Co-dependence means recognising that we're all in this together. It means extending credit lines when suppliers are going through a rough patch. It means paying proper wages to employees and not manipulating EPS to inflate executive rewards. It means recognising that every wage you pay and every supplier you contract has a long tail, meaning that thousands more rely on your actions than you may think.

At a micro level your business is likely to undergo profound change. You'll probably see a reduction in global travel and business conferences. You may even have a rethink on the role of offices, certainly reducing their overall capacity. Does everyone really have to be in the same place at the same time all the time? Perhaps you'll reconsider the effectiveness of open plan working. Or even think about how to increase productivity by working smarter – fewer hours, less travel, more technology.

The lockdown has thrown up multiple issues. None of us knows the right answer. Indeed, there won't be one. Your job as a leader is not to provide certainty. It is to work with your teams and inspire them to generate flexible solutions.

Now is your opportunity to be more purposeful and collaborative. You should be more joined up and use whole systems thinking, involving your staff, customers and suppliers. There is an interdependence in every aspect of business, in effect, a shared economy.

Perhaps it is time for a radical rethink of your priorities.

How do you want to be remembered over the lockdown? Is it as the leader who steadied the ship? Or perhaps as the leader who cut the cost base in order to stay afloat?

> What if the lockdown turned out to be the best thing that happened to you

What if, rather than seeing the lockdown as a crisis, you saw it as an opportunity to re-set and re-think how work works. It can provide a real opportunity to renew. After all, there's no point in fighting the last war. Things have moved on rapidly.

And as a business leader you can be at the forefront of making real change. Nobody wants to go back to exactly as it was before.

The pandemic changed a lot – physically and emotionally.

So now is the time to look forward.

> Business and society need to be:
>
> - More purposeful
> - More adaptive
> - And more collaborative

There's going to be greater expectation for a more joined-up society. There's going to be lots of opportunity and appetite for change. The businesses that succeed will be those that are the most adaptable and flexible.

It's time for reinvention and rethinking. It's time to be radical.

So, don't waste a good crisis.

Leading from home will prove to have provided you with many challenges. But the biggest will be to change your mindset, your attitudes, your actions and your behaviours.

And the new more flexible, more resilient and more adaptable version of you will be the leader who can make the most of the new environment.

Which means that there are real reasons to be optimistic. And that's a good thing for everyone.

ABOUT THE AUTHOR

Tim Johns is a consultant and coach specialising in leadership, communications and change.

@oratotim

www.oratoconsulting.co.uk

Printed in Great Britain
by Amazon